discovermore

World Religions

What Is Islam?

Dwight Morris

Britannica Educational Publishing

IN ASSOCIATION WITH

Published in 2026 by Britannica Educational Publishing (a trademark of Encyclopædia Britannica, Inc.) in association with The Rosen Publishing Group, Inc.
2544 Clinton Street, Buffalo, NY 14224

Distributed exclusively by Rosen Publishing.
To see additional Britannica Educational Publishing titles, go to rosenpublishing.com.

Portions of this work were originally authored by Tayyaba Syed and published as *Islam*. All new material in this edition was authored by Dwight Morris.

Editor: Greg Roza
Book Design: Michael Flynn

Photo Credits: Cover Romolo Tavani/Shutterstock.com; (series background) Dai Yim/Shutterstock.com; p. 4 Erico setiawan/Shutterstock.com; p. 5 Nagel Photography/Shutterstock.com; p. 6 ahmad.jaa/Shutterstock.com; p. 7 PeopleImages.com - Yuri A/Shutterstock.com; p. 8 Robert Hoetink/Shutterstock.com; p. 9 ventdusud/Shutterstock.com; p. 10 Sener Dagasan/Shutterstock.com; p. 11 Sony Herdiana/Shutterstock.com; p. 12 Renata Sedmakova/Shutterstock.com; p. 13 khair mispan/Shutterstock.com; p. 15 (top) Billion Photos/Shutterstock.com; p. 15 (bottom) Drazen Zigic/Shutterstock.com; p. 16 Magic Orb Studio/Shutterstock.com; p. 17 leshiy985/Shutterstock.com; p. 18 Vuk Kostic/Shutterstock.com; p. 19 Mistervlad/Shutterstock.com; p. 21 (top) Drazen Zigic/Shutterstock.com; p. 21 (bottom) Project XYZ/Shutterstock.com; p. 23 (top) teera.noisakran/Shutterstock.com; p. 23 (bottom) Anas-Mohammed/Shutterstock.com; p. 24 Habs Photography/Shutterstock.com; p. 25 imrankadir/Shutterstock.com; p. 26 https://commons.wikimedia.org/wiki/File:Taking_of_Laghouat_1852.jpg; p. 27 https://commons.wikimedia.org/wiki/File:Portrait_of_Ruhollah_Khomeini.jpg; p. 28 Cris Faga/Shutterstock.com; p. 29 Drazen Zigic/Shutterstock.com.

Cataloging-in-Publication Data

Names: Morris, Dwight.
Title: What is Islam? / Dwight Morris.
Description: New York : Britannica Educational Publishing, in association with Rosen Educational Services, 2026. | Series: Discover more: world religions | Includes glossary and index.
Identifiers: ISBN 9781641904643 (library bound) | ISBN 9781641904636 (pbk) | ISBN 9781641904650 (ebook)
Subjects: LCSH: Islam--Juvenile literature.
Classification: LCC BP161.3 M677 2026 | DDC 297--dc23

Manufactured in the United States of America

CPSIA Compliance Information: Batch #CSBRIT26. For further information contact Rosen Publishing at 1-800-237-9932.

Contents

The Will of Allah

Islam was founded in the seventh century CE by Muhammad in what is now Saudi Arabia. Followers of Islam are called Muslims. Like Christianity and Judaism, Islam is **monotheistic**. It teaches that there is only one God, called Allah, and that he created the world. The Arabic word "Islam" means "submission" or "surrender." Muslims strive to live a life obeying the will of Allah.

Indonesia in Southeast Asia has the largest Muslim population in the world with more than 242 million followers.

There are nearly 4.5 million Muslims in the United States.

Today, Islam is the second largest religion in the world. It has about 1.6 billion followers worldwide, or one-fifth of the world's population. Most Muslims live in southern and central Asia, North Africa, and the Middle East. However, there are Muslims all over the world.

WORD WISE

MONOTHEISTIC RELIGIONS HONOR A SINGLE GOD. A POLYTHEISTIC RELIGION IS ONE THAT HONORS MORE THAN ONE GOD.

Islamic Beliefs

Muslims believe that the Koran, the holy book of Islam, is the word of God as told to the **prophet** Muhammad. At the center of Islam is the shahadah, or a statement of faith. "There is no God but Allah, and Muhammad is the prophet of Allah." It states the oneness of God and the belief that Muhammad was the last prophet in a long line of prophets. Muslims believe that God is kind and fair and that God created the world and will one day judge humankind.

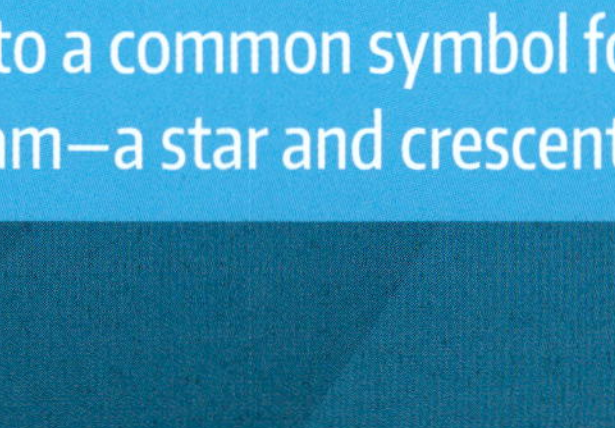

The shahadah is etched onto a common symbol for Islam—a star and crescent.

Wherever they are, Muslims pray at five specific times each day. This could be in a mosque, at home, or even public places such as markets.

Muslims practice their faith not just as a religion but also as a way of life. Five duties, called the five pillars of Islam, are expected of every Muslim. The first pillar, the shahadah, or statement of faith, is the most important.

The second pillar of Islam is prayer. Muslims pray five times a day: at dawn, midday, midafternoon, sunset, and before going to bed. Before prayer, Muslims wash their hands, feet, and face.

WORD WISE

A PROPHET IS A RELIGIOUS FIGURE WHO DECLARES PUBLICLY A MESSAGE THAT ONE BELIEVES HAS COME FROM GOD OR A GOD.

A person called the muezzin calls for prayers and chants from a raised platform or minaret tower at the mosque, the place of worship. A person called the imam stands at the front of the mosque and leads the congregation in prayer. The congregation lines up in rows behind the imam. There are no seats in a mosque. During prayer, Muslims stand, kneel, and bow down. On Fridays, communities gather at the mosque for special prayers. They pray, listen to parts of the Koran, and hear a sermon.

An imam speaks to Muslims in a mosque in the Netherlands.

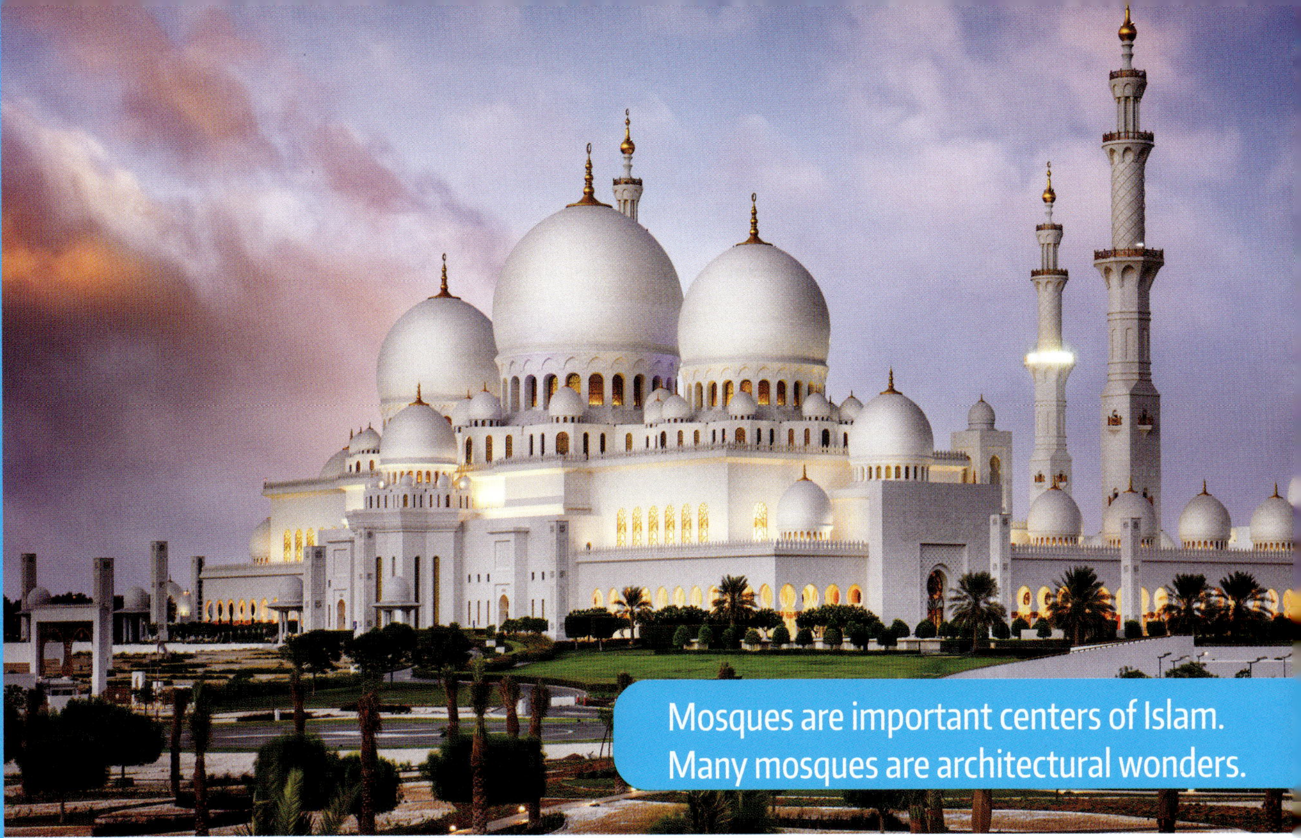

Mosques are important centers of Islam. Many mosques are architectural wonders.

The third pillar of Islam is charity, or money given to the poor and needy of the community. The fourth pillar is to fast, or go without food, from sunrise to sunset during the holy month of Ramadan. The fifth pillar is to make a pilgrimage to the holy city of Mecca in Saudi Arabia at least once. A pilgrimage is a holy journey.

Consider This

When Muslims pray they kneel and face the holy city of Mecca. Why do you think they do this?

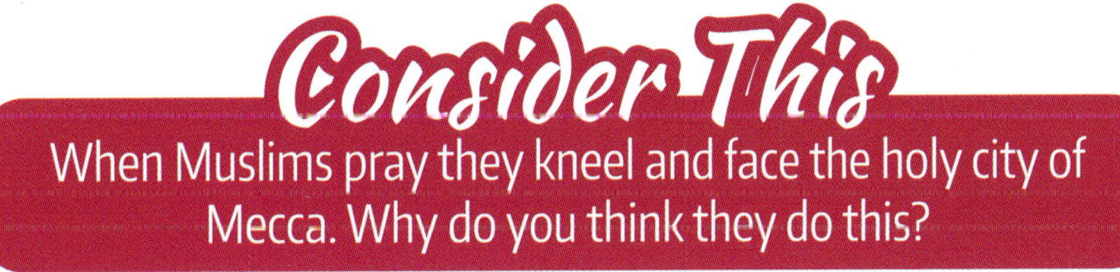

The Prophet Muhammad

Muhammad was born in the Arabian town of Mecca in about 570 CE. Muhammad's father died before he was born, and Muhammad's mother died when he was six. He was raised by his grandfather and later by his uncle. Muhammad grew up poor but worked very hard. First he worked as a shepherd. Later he became a well-known tradesman.

Many Muslims believe that Muhammad and Allah should not be depicted in artistic form. This spelling of Muhammad's name in Arabic calligraphy is more often used to represent him.

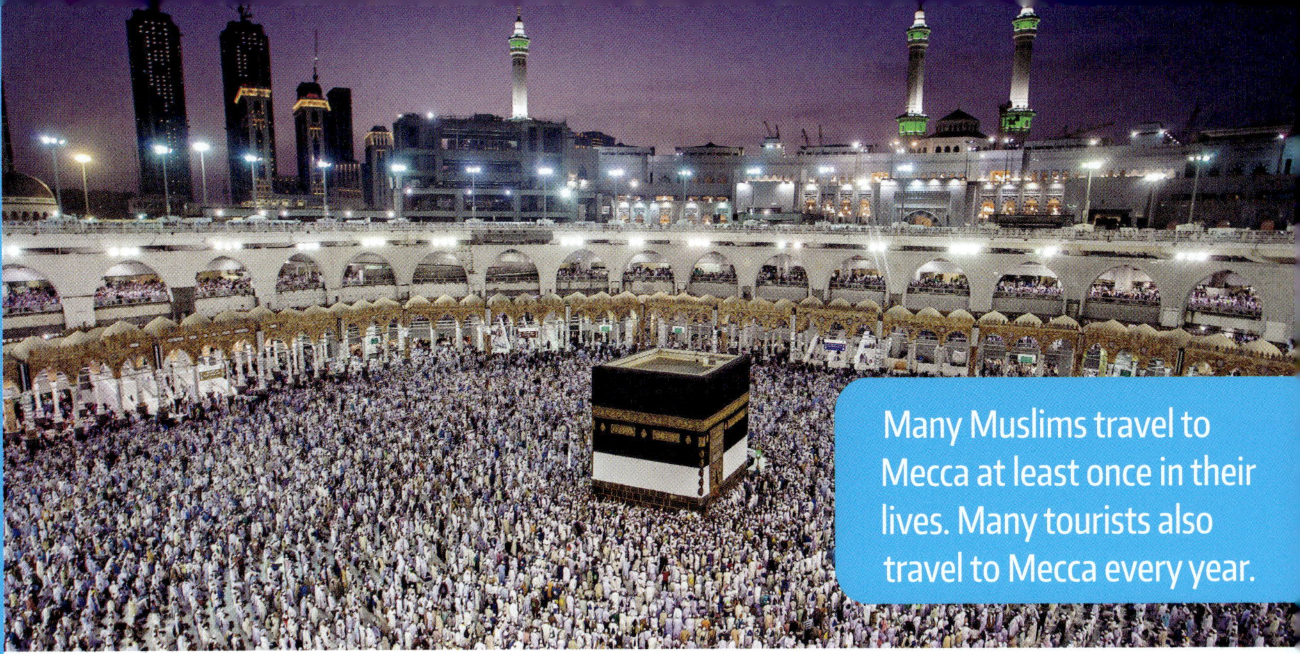

Many Muslims travel to Mecca at least once in their lives. Many tourists also travel to Mecca every year.

When Muhammad was about twenty-five years old, he married a rich, older woman named Khadijah. Their marriage helped Muhammad become wealthy and important in his community. Muhammad and Khadijah had six children. Two of their sons died when they were young. Of their four daughters, the best known is Fatima. Although many men at the time had more than one wife, Khadijah was Muhammad's only wife until she died. Muhammad took several wives after the death of Khadijah.

Consider This

Do you think the circumstances of Muhammad's life may have influenced the five pillars of Islam? How so?

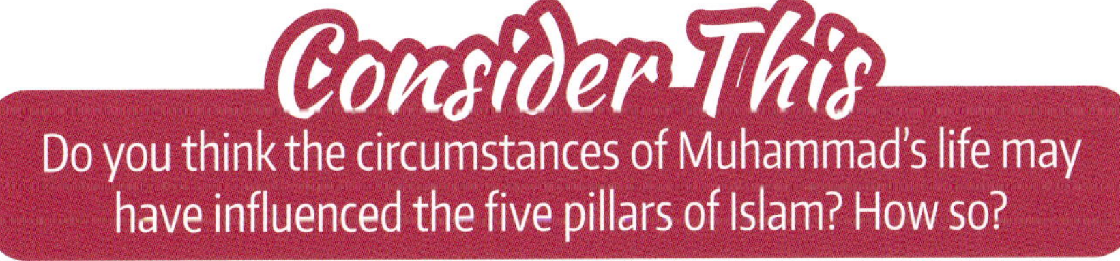

Muhammad sometimes climbed a mountain near Mecca where sat in a cave to **meditate**. One night in the year 610 CE, Muhammad was in this cave when he received what he believed was a message from God. Muhammad had a vision of the angel Gabriel, who told Muhammad there was one God, not many gods, as most Arabs believed. The angel also told Muhammad that Allah had chosen him as a prophet.

The angel Gabriel appears in the Jewish Bible, the Christian Bible, as well as the Koran.

Muslim pilgrims visit the cave where Allah spoke to Muhammad.

Throughout his life, Muhammad continued to receive messages that he believed came from God. In about 613 Muhammad began preaching the new ideas that had been revealed to him. Many people in Mecca were against the new ideas. Muhammad worried that his enemies might hurt him and his followers. He encouraged his followers to move to the nearby city of Medina. Muhammad's trip to Medina is known as the Hegira. Muhammad himself reached Medina on September 24, 622, which is considered the starting date for the history of Islam.

WORD WISE

TO MEDITATE MEANS TO SPEND TIME QUIETLY THINKING AND REFLECTING. RELIGIOUS MEDITATION MAY INCLUDE DEEP BREATHING, FOCUSED THOUGHTS, AND CHANTING.

The Holy Book of Islam

Muhammad shared the words God spoke to him with his followers. His followers then wrote them down, and these writings became the Koran, the holy book of Islam. The word "Koran" is an English version of the Arabic word Qur'an, which means "recitation."

Muslims believe the answers to all religious, social, and legal issues are in the Koran. One important subject in the Koran is resurrection, or rising from the dead. Other topics include angels and devils, heaven and hell, and foods that are forbidden to eat, such as pork. There are also chapters about marriage and divorce laws. Other sections tell the duties of parents to their children, of masters to their servants, and of the rich to the poor.

Muslims believe that everything Muhammad said and did was inspired by Allah. Because of that, his followers wrote down many of his words and actions, which serve as an additional guide for Muslims. These writings are called Hadith.

The Koran is made up of 114 chapters called suras. Each sura has a prayer and verses.

compare and contrast

How is the Koran similar to or different from other religious texts, such as the Torah of Judaism or the Christian Bible?

All Muslims memorize short sections of the Koran to recite in their daily prayers.

The Spread of Islam

After Muhammad's death in 632 CE, Muslims disagreed as to who should lead them. Muhammad's son-in-law 'Ali became the Muslim leader, or caliph, in 656. But he was murdered in 661. Some Muslims thought that 'Ali's descendants should be their leaders. This group formed the Shi'ah branch of Islam and are called Shi'ites. The Muslims who disagreed formed the Sunnah branch.

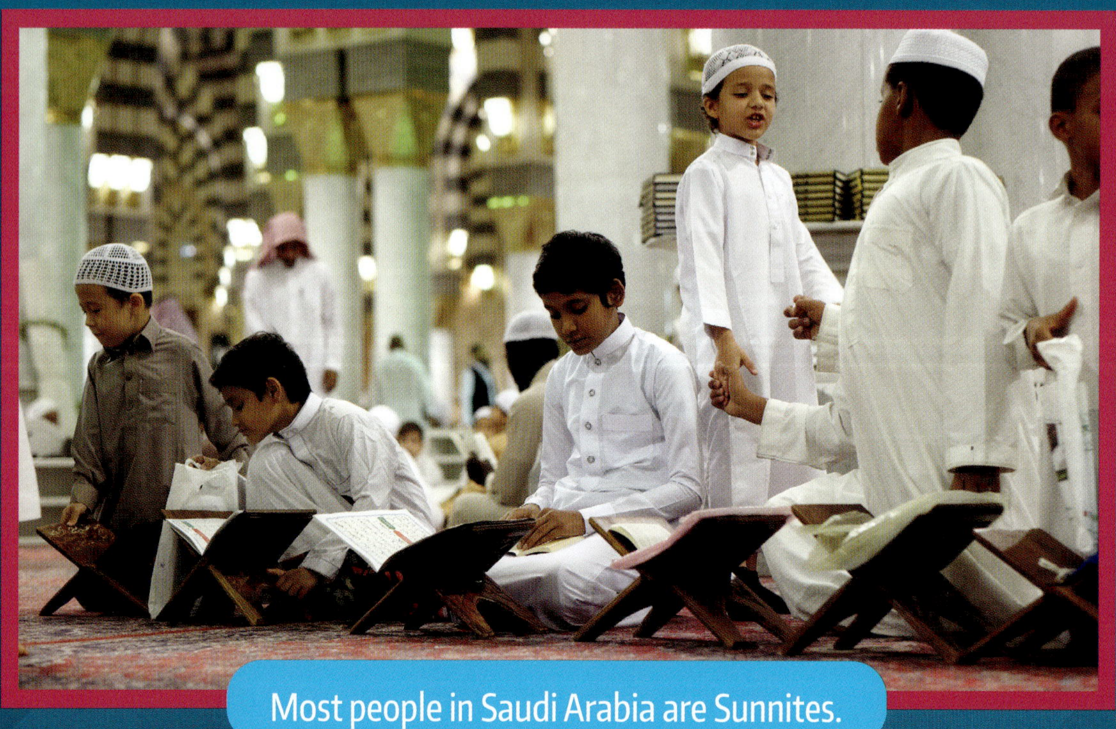

Most people in Saudi Arabia are Sunnites.

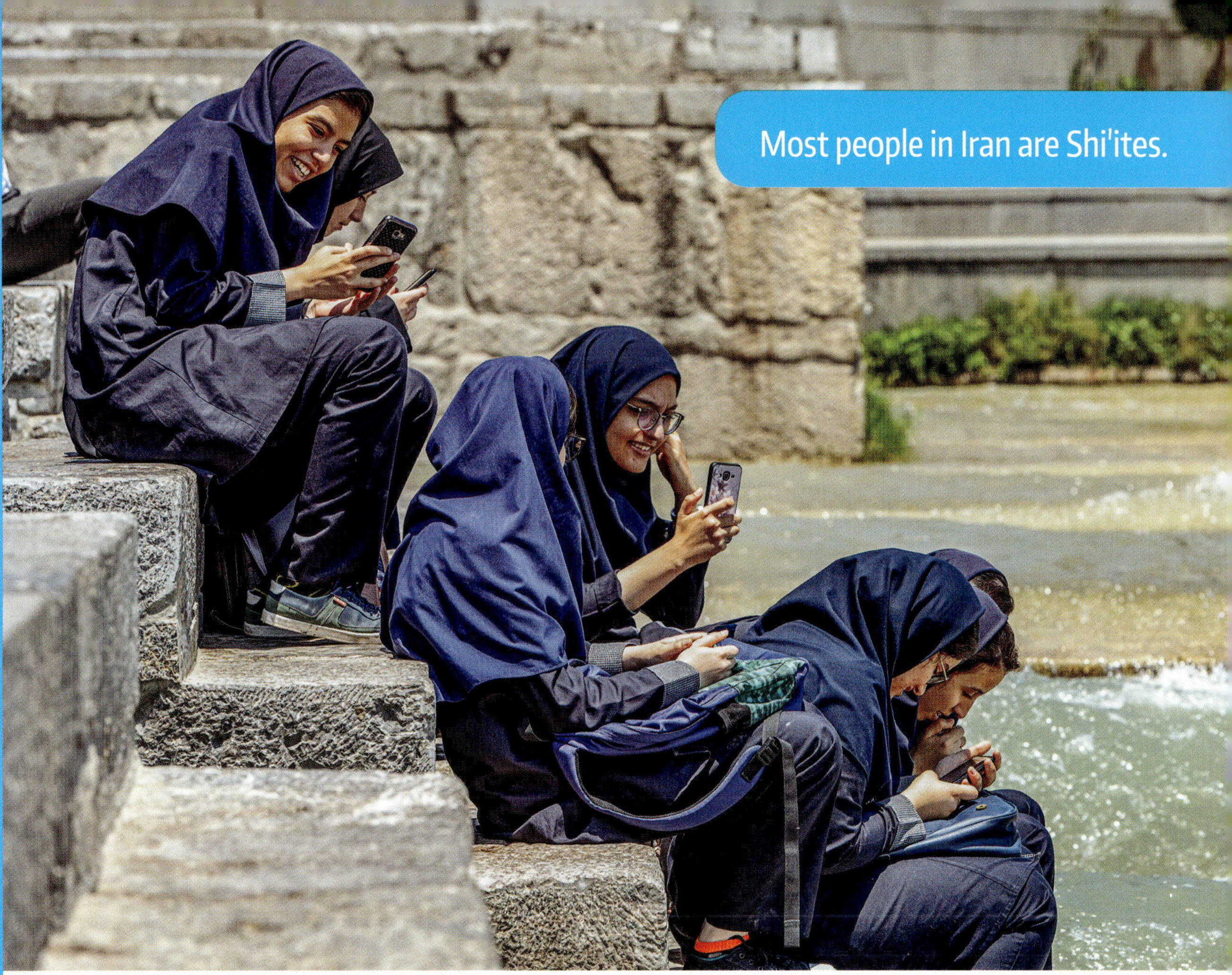

Most people in Iran are Shi'ites.

Most Muslims are Sunnites, or followers of the Sunnah branch. They are known as traditional Muslims. They follow the sayings of Muhammad and emphasize community.

Consider This

Why do you think religions, such as Islam and Christianity, have different branches or schools of thought?

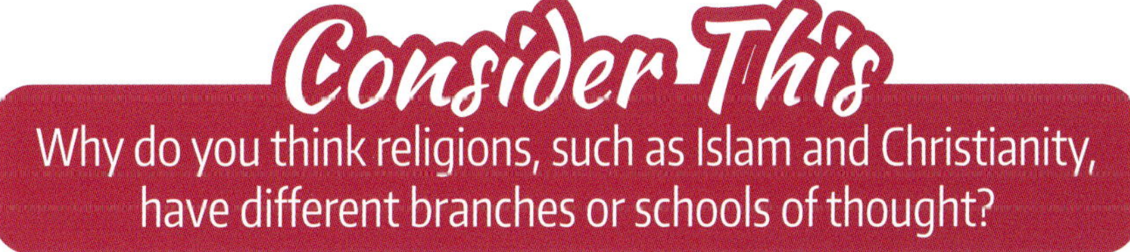

Shi'ites—the members of the smaller Shi'ah branch—believe that the truths of the Koran are revealed only through the imam. Interpretations by other people are not accepted. For this reason Shi'ites are not as open to other views as Sunnites are.

During the 600s and 700s, Islam spread far beyond Arabia, from the western Mediterranean region to Central Asia. Holy wars called jihads were fought to conquer new lands and spread Islam.

The Crusades were a series of wars in the Middle Ages. Christian and Muslim armies fought for control of the Holy Land, located primarily on the eastern coast of the Mediterranean Sea.

Istanbul, Turkey, has been an important center of Islamic culture since the time of the Ottoman Empire. The Hagia Sophia Grand Mosque in Istanbul, shown here, was originally a Christian church.

In the Middle East a group called the Seljuks would not let Christians visit holy sites in the land they controlled. Over the next two centuries, Muslims and Christians fought over the **Holy Land** in a series of wars known as the Crusades. In the 1200s another group of Muslim Turks, the Ottomans, began a powerful Islamic empire. For hundreds of years, the Ottomans ruled over North Africa, the Middle East, and southeastern Europe.

WORD WISE

THE HOLY LAND IS A PART OF THE MIDDLE EAST THAT IS SACRED TO THREE MAJOR RELIGIONS: JUDAISM, CHRISTIANITY, AND ISLAM. IT LIES BETWEEN THE JORDAN RIVER AND THE MEDITERRANEAN SEA.

Muslim Holidays

'Id al-Fitr and 'Id al-Adha are the two major religious holidays for Muslims. 'Id al-Fitr happens at the end of Ramadan, which is the ninth month of the Islamic calendar. Ramadan marks the time when Muhammad received the words of the Koran. Muslims observe Ramadan by praying, reading the Koran, and fasting. Muslims believe their past sins will be forgiven if they participate in Ramadan.

During Ramadan, most Muslims must fast during daylight hours. Small children, old people, and sick people may eat. After sunset, Muslims break their fast with prayer and festive meals. Called iftar, these meals are shared with friends and family. After meals, people visit other friends and relatives. The twenty-seventh night of Ramadan is celebrated as the Night of Power, or Lailat al Kadr. Muslims spend extra hours in prayer then. On that night, it is said, Allah revealed the Koran to Muhammad.

Iftar meals begin with dates, which is how Muhammad is said to have broke his fast many years ago.

compare and contrast

Ramadan may happen in any season of the year. That's because the Islamic calendar is based on the moon. Can you think of any other holidays that occur on a different day each year?

This family reads from the Koran together during Ramadan.

Muslims celebrate 'Id al-Fitr, or the Festival of Breaking Fast, when Ramadan ends. 'Id al-Fitr occurs during the first three days of Shawwal, the tenth month of the Islamic calendar. Muslims begin the festival by praying together at dawn on the first day. Later, families gather to enjoy special meals and sweets. Children wear new clothes, and gifts are exchanged. People also visit the graves of relatives. Some cities hold large ceremonies outdoors.

The holiday 'Id al-Adha is held each year to mark the end of the hajj, the pilgrimage to Mecca. Its name means the Festival of Sacrifice. It commemorates a story in the Koran in which God asks Ibrahim (also known as Abraham) to sacrifice his son. Ibrahim prepares to do so, but then God lets him sacrifice a ram instead. 'Id al-Adha lasts for four days. Some families sacrifice an animal and divide the meat among family members, friends, neighbors, and the poor. It is a time for prayer, visiting with friends and family, and giving gifts.

Muslims in Thailand gather on the morning of 'Id al-Fitr to pray together.

compare and contrast

How are the holidays of 'Id al-Fitr and 'Id al-Adha different from or similar to each other?

These children in Palestine are celebrating 'Id al-Adha with a clown!

Pilgrimage to Mecca

Muslims must make a pilgrimage to Mecca, Saudi Arabia, at least once in their lifetime. This is called the hajj, the fifth pillar of Islam. Hajj begins on the eighth day of Dhu al-Hijjah (the last month of the Islamic year) and ends on the thirteenth day. About two million people perform the hajj each year. Every Muslim who is physically and financially able must make the pilgrimage.

The Ka'bah is about 50 feet high (15.2 m), and it is about 35 feet (10.7 m) by 40 feet (12.2 m) at its base. The Black Stone is built into the eastern wall of the Ka'bah. Muslims believe it was part of the earliest Ka'bah structure.

Muslims try to touch the Ka'bah during the hajj to Mecca. This can be difficult with thousands of people in the same place at the same time.

Before reaching Mecca, pilgrims enter a state of holiness and purity called ihram. In this state, pilgrims wear white and do not cut their hair or nails. When they reach Mecca, pilgrims walk seven times around a sacred **shrine** called the Ka'bah in the Great Mosque. They try to touch or kiss the Black Stone in the Ka'bah. Outside of Mecca, pilgrims visit the site of Muhammad's last sermon and ask God's forgiveness. It is the most important part of the hajj. At the end of the hajj, pilgrims return to Mecca and circle the Ka'bah again before leaving the city.

WORD WISE

A SHRINE IS A PLACE OR AN OBJECT THAT IS CONSIDERED SACRED, OR HOLY. SHRINES ARE OFTEN PLACES FOR PRAYER AND OTHER FORMS OF WORSHIP.

Islam Today

Western powers established colonies in Muslim nations to trade with the people living there starting in the 1800s. Islamic leaders lost political power, but Muslims gathered together more tightly as a community in response to **colonization**. In the 1900s this sense of unity helped many Muslim countries fight for and win political independence.

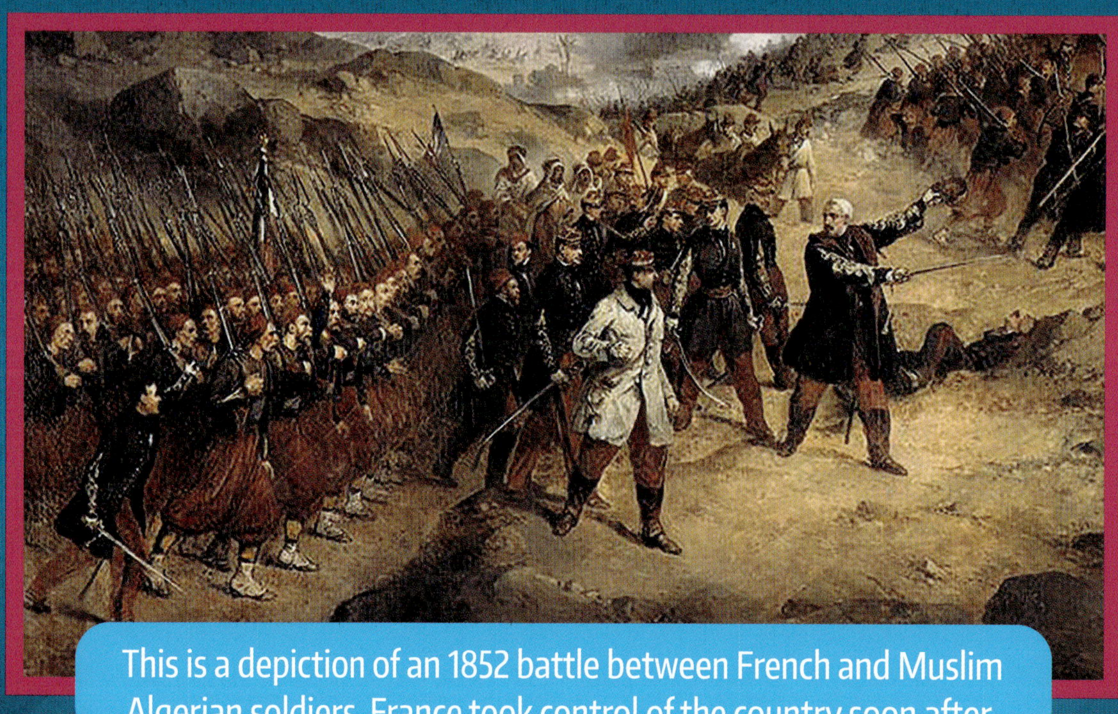

This is a depiction of an 1852 battle between French and Muslim Algerian soldiers. France took control of the country soon after.

After the revolution in Iran, Ruhollah Khomeini became the first supreme leader of the country. He ruled until his death in 1989. Khomeini's government enforced strict Muslim laws and banned Western influences.

In the late 1900s Islam became one of the fastest growing world religions. Some Muslims have resisted the influence of the West, which they view as leading to a loss of traditional Muslim values. In Iran a revolution brought Islamic religious leaders to power in 1979. Today, Shi'ism is the national religion of Iran.

WORD WISE

COLONIZATION IS THE ACT OF A NATION TAKING CONTROL OF A DISTANT TERRITORY, REGARDLESS IF THAT TERRITORY ALREADY HAS A GROUP OF PEOPLE WITH LEADERS OF THEIR OWN.

The world's mostly Muslim countries form a long band from the Atlantic Ocean across North Africa, the Middle East, and South and Central Asia. Indonesia, an island nation in the Indian and Pacific oceans, has more Muslims than any other country. Islam is the most popular religion in more than thirty countries.

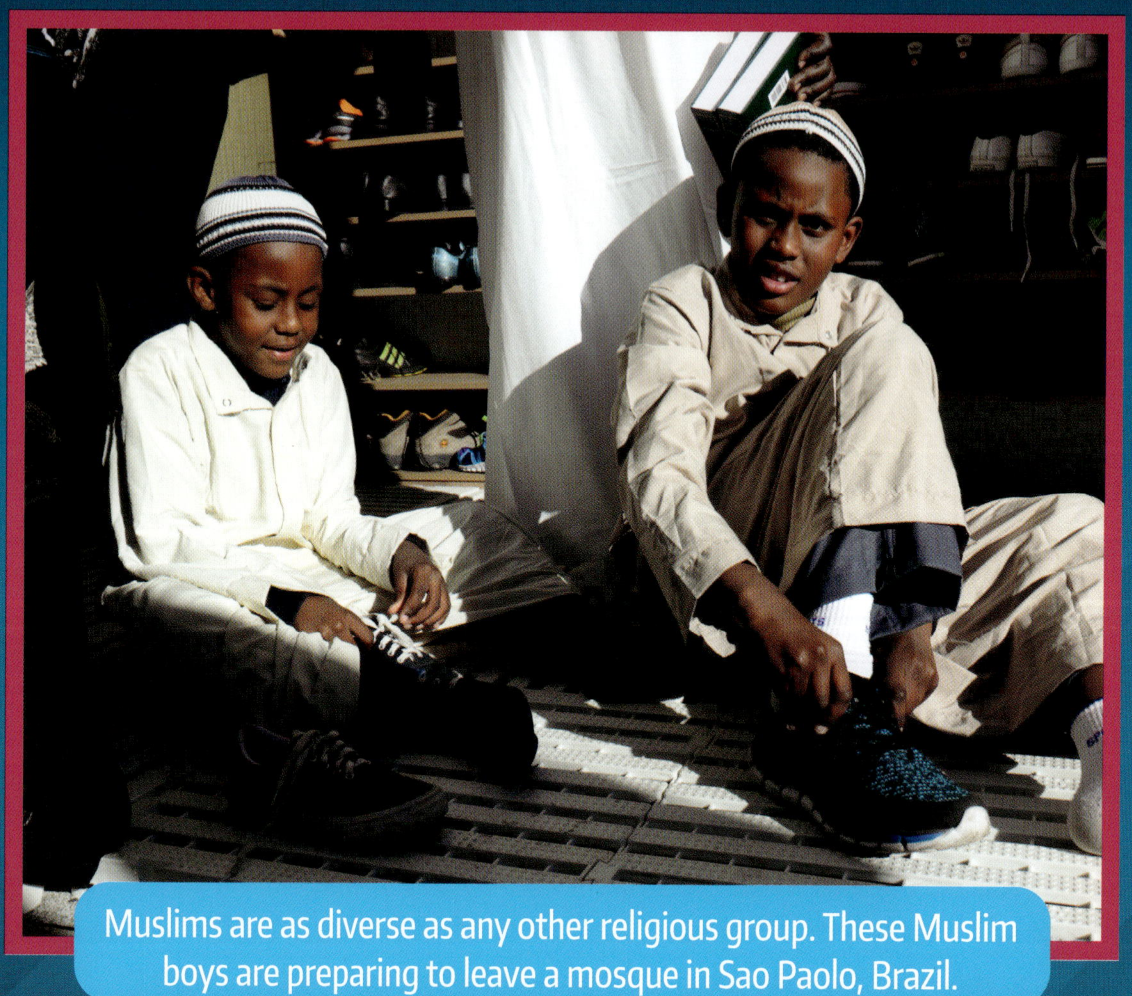

Muslims are as diverse as any other religious group. These Muslim boys are preparing to leave a mosque in Sao Paolo, Brazil.

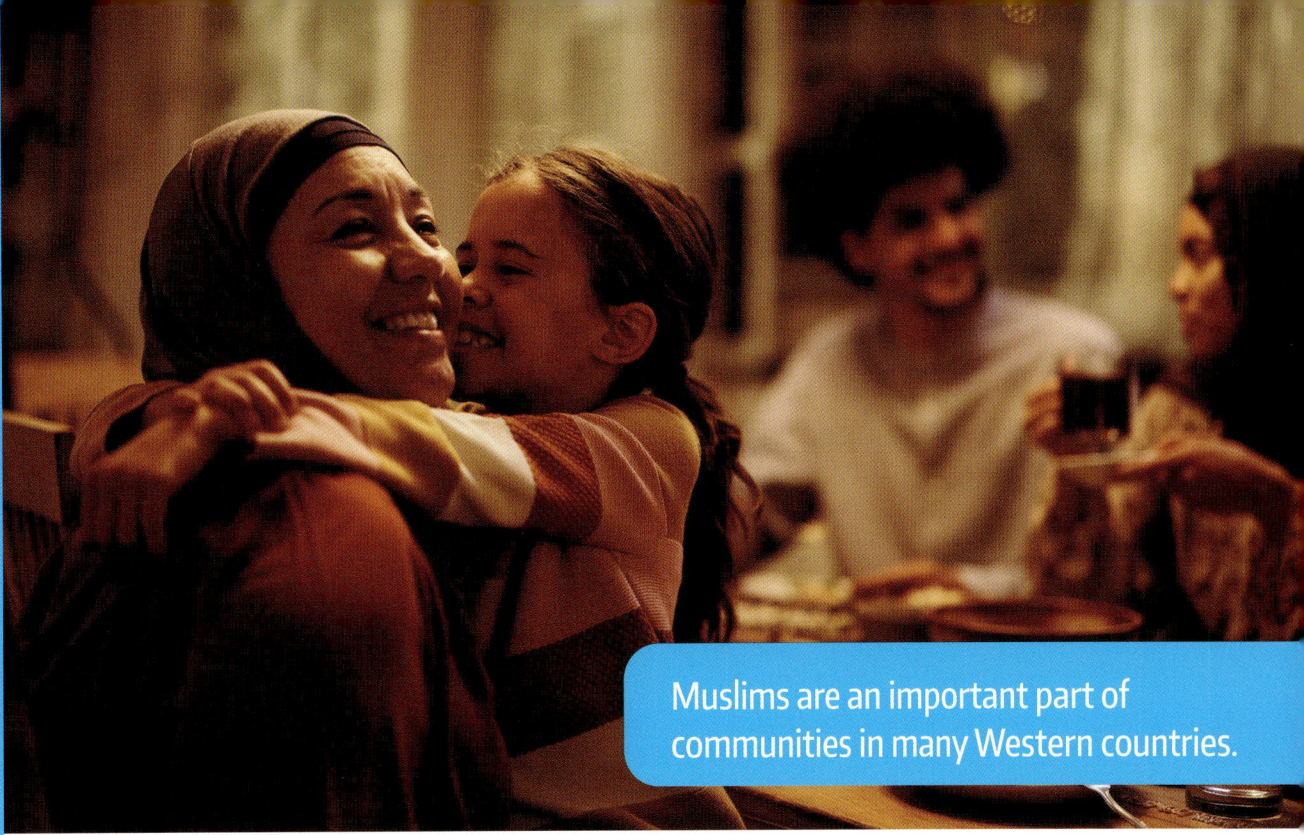

Muslims are an important part of communities in many Western countries.

Muslims also live in other countries throughout the world, including North America. Muslims in North America come from many different backgrounds. Despite the differences in their backgrounds, Muslims around the world view themselves as one community united by their belief in Allah and the teachings of his prophet Muhammad.

Consider This

How might the hajj pilgrimage help maintain the link between Muslims from all over the world?

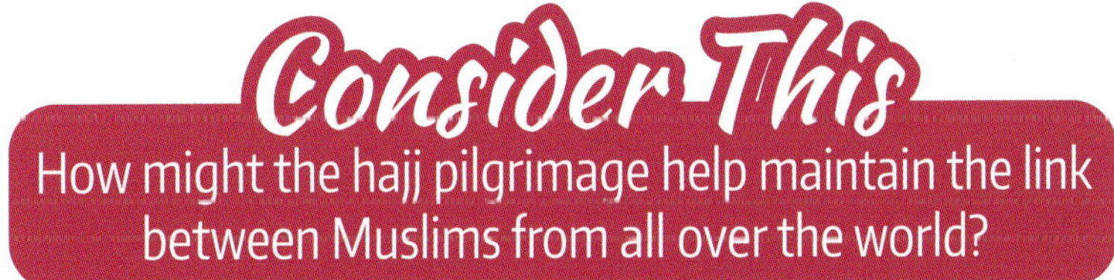

Glossary

Arabia Peninsula of southwest Asia including Saudi Arabia, Yemen, Oman, and the Persian Gulf States.
calligraphy Beautiful handwriting.
chant To speak with little or no change in tone.
charity The giving of aid to the poor and suffering.
devout Having a strong belief in a religion.
fast To go without eating.
Holy Land Part of the Middle East that is sacred to Judaism, Christianity, and Islam and includes the city of Jerusalem.
memorize To learn by heart.
minaret A tall tower of a mosque from which a muezzin calls worshipers to prayer.
mosque A Muslim place of worship.
pilgrimage A journey to a shrine or holy place to worship.
pillar A supporting or important part of something.
prophet A person who shares a message that he or she believes has come from God.
sacrifice Killing an animal as an offering to God.
sermon A talk that teaches a lesson, usually given by a religious leader.
shrine A place or an object that is considered sacred or holy.

For More Information

Books

Golkar, Golriz. *Islamic Festivals and Traditions.* Broomfield, CO: Pebble Books, 2025.

Noor, Little. *The Five Pillars of Islam.* Independantly published, 2025.

Websites

Early Islamic World
www.ducksters.com/history/islam
Read more about Islam and it's followers.

Islam 4 Kids
www.islam4kids.org
This website has many chances to learn more about Islam, including games, stories, videos, and more.

Publisher's note to educators and parents: Our editors have carefully reviewed these websites to ensure that they are suitable for students. Many websites change frequently, however, and we cannot guarantee that a site's future contents will continue to meet our high standards of quality and educational value. Be advised that students should be closely supervised whenever they access the internet.

Index